Graceful Poetry

Grace Rapavi

Lake Superior Publishing, Wisconsin

First Edition

The Place We Share

The grassy meadow from here to there,
The paths to the place we share,
The open fields, the tall thin wheat,
The soft earth under my bare feet,
The chirping birds, the sunlight shining,
And brushing bushels I am reclining,
The open air, the flowers in flock,
The garden with dirt so fertilized in stock,
The clear sparkling water that flows from the
stream,
The beautiful sunset that gloriously gleams,
The tall apple trees now at their best,
With haste I run from side to side and in His
arms, there do I rest.

Music of Our Hearts

Soft cries we hear from birds within,
We feel their sorrow in a different perspective.
How they live, how they sing,
How they express themselves in a positive
way.
When they are sad their song seems less
fluent,
And their eyes view down at the fragrant earth.
When they are frightened they fly to the nearest
shelter
And refuge as where they can rely on help, not
hurt.
But when they are happy, that's a different
story,
They fly up to the highest tree and sing for
hours without end,
And exclaim by giving us fluent, soft, and
angelic music
To take in on that cool spring day, when
everything started
To come a bloom again.

Spring

The birds chirp,
The butterflies flitter,
And their magical wings seem to give off glitter.
The bunnies hop,
The deer prance,
And it almost seems like a dance.
The roses in the garden smell so sweet,
And the rippling waters give off a soft beat.

Spring Wishes

Beyond a meadow of flowers,
So far, the eye can't see,
Is a village upon a cliff,
As mountains surround thee.
The green grass sprung so high,
The clouds came as a mist,
And this village full of beauty,
Became my earnest wish.

Winter Switch

Deep within the mountains, where the snow
began to melt,
A beautiful feeling came about me,
One I've never felt.
The icy snow made clear blue water, the clouds
became a mist.
The swiftness of the hilltops,
And the wind- I felt a switch,
This beauty changed my life,
A calm fresh sight,
And as the Lord looks down,
He'll see His finest delight.

A Dreary Delight

It was a chilly morning,
The mist as thick as fog,
And the mud near the green trees,
To cause an ugly bog.
But even this sorrowful sight,
One you'd never wish,
This is the beauty that- even you can't switch.
You see this dreary day,
Will soon turn around,
One time, another day,
At this place,
Will turn your frown upside down.

April Blessings

Where the trees grow tall,
And the green leaves start to show,
The beauty you've been awaiting,
Will be here sooner than you know,
White flowers guard the pathway,
And green is all around.
This beauty is so peaceful,
A peaceful, beautiful, sound!

May Flowers

From this mighty view,
You could clearly see,
The hilltops all about you,
And after, a deep blue sea,
The flowers kneel in praise,
As they multiply the beauty evermore,
This is everlasting beauty,
One I truly wish for.

A Fresh Sight

The water was so cleansing,
So pure and blue,
The sky matched its color,
It was beautifully true,
The water made the shapes,
Deep within the rocks,
I took this gorgeous sight,
And in my heart it's locked.

Cloudy Sunshine

At this particular place,
The clouds drew a bit dark,
But as the day went on,
There was a mighty start.
A start of calm blue waters,
That passed beyond the shore,
And yet, the greenery behind it,
The trees behind on the shore,
The island in the middle,
Kept me going more.
This place took my heart,
And wrapped it up with beauty,
This particular sight,
Has clearly shown love truly.

This Day

This day I wake with gladness,
This morning I wake with Your joy,
I feel Your blessings reaching out,
For my heart and soul.

This evening I hear Your voice,
This evening I remember this day,
And how when I fell,
You did answer, and did not wander away.

This night I recall my day through,
It seems as if I were alone,
I will now always remember,
That You were there through the storm.

I See

The cedars all bending in a row,
The singing robin,
The black big crow,
I see Your blessing, big and small,
Throughout the world, and live with awe.

With all of These

The sun shines gently through the trees,
The birds in air stretch out their wings,
The trees do bend and show their leaves,
God displays beauty with all of these.

What I Saw

I saw the sun and its bright yellow beams,
I saw the colorful crisp leaves on the trees,
I glide through the water as it ripples past,
I lay within the tall thick grass.

Starry Sky

The sky is starry, filled with light,
Which I do enjoy, Your creatures who come out at night,
Be filled with joy,
I find my place of love, Your blessings flow,
And those who don't love,
Will never surely know.

Swaying in the Breeze

The stream runs slowly, gently by,
Creating a soft, sweet sound,
The willow trees swing with ease,
Nearly touching the damp, cool ground.

Your Secret

And how I see Your beauty is a secret to
mankind,
A modest vow, a way of life,
Your work for me, my words for You,
Your will be done, mine given to Thee.

Through the Raindrops

Through the raindrops Your love comes for my thirst,
Through the flowers, my heart blooms and bursts,
Through the meadow, through the trees,
My heart, Lord, flies and grows with your wonders,
And in it all, bestows an everlasting peace.

Ever New

How I see Thee ever true,
How You love me ever new,
How I see Thee, though my path,
How You heal me through the pain,
How I love Thee ever true,
How You see me, ever new.

My Every Joy

A beauty, a tear,
A gift, a fear,
A triumph, a pain,
Through the trials,
What love I gain.

A sadness, a joy,
A heart, an implore,
A sign, a wondering sight,
You alone Lord,
Are my delight.

A victory, a defeat,
A battle, an army fleet,
A cry, not to ignore,
I will win for you,
My every joy.

What You Really Mean to Me

Friendship is a special gift,
And to help one another,
To complement and uplift,
Someone to talk to,
A helpful person I can rely,
A person I can trust,
A person I can with, laugh and cry.

Yours

Being your friend has meant so much to me,
Your impact in my life
Is more than you can see,
A friend to share my feelings,
A person who truly cares,
Your thoughtfulness and trust,
A love almost too much to bear.

More than You Know

Your friendship is so special,
More than you ever could know,
You're the best friend I could ever have,
And I mean that ever so.

Lighten the Sky

O how thy majesties lighten the sky,
After a day of rain and storm,
Oh how thy blessings ever grow,
Like a flower about to bloom,
O how thy mercies ever flow,
Like a stream up to the shore,
O how thy servants ever serve,
And praise You all the more.

When I Sing

Created in His image,
I am beautiful ever so,
More importantly inside than outside,
Through Your love it ever shows.
Created in His image,
My talents are from Him,
To praise You in everything,
In song, too, when I sing.

More than the Sunshine

You are more than I make of You,
More than I can see,
More than I think of You,
Lovely Thy ever be,
More than the beauty of a sunset,
Or of a moon lighted lake,
More than the sunshine,
Much more than can I take.

Rings Anew

A special gift from Thine own hands,
A song to praise Him,
O how what grand,
To see Thy glory shining through,
Thy mountains jumping,
So rings anew.

Towards the Sun

I saw a flower in a field,
It's petals toward the sun,
The dew ran down it's delicate stem,
It was cared for and loved,
It made me think of Your care for me,
And how You never leave,
If only me, a simple melody,
Would have as much gave,
A stream of water flowing by,
It's crystal fluid reflects the sky,
A hill that reached up to the clouds,
I hear the wind and its swerving sounds,
The tall grass, the fertile dirt,
Tall trees, which bees inside insert.

Never Look Down

Up in the sky the sun shines bright,
The moon reflects thy glorious delight,
Down below deep in the sea,
I find what love You give to me,
And in between, where I stand right now,
I dare not ever look down,
For in due time I will look up and see,
You looking lovingly at me.

Your Love not Far

Protect this child as it sleeps,
Catch it's tears when it weeps,
Hold it close to Your heart,
Let it see Your love not far.

Hold it's hand as it runs,
Give it words for it's tongue,
Let Your beauty it shall see,
This life is a mystery.

A smile that does ever glow,
Upon this small life You bestow,
Flowing hair caught in the wind,
Truly a loving friend.

A heart to feel Your unending love,
To capture Your glorious face above,
To remember me, a child thou art,
And ever love You from the start.

Thy Love Shall Sing

To see the pain You must endure,
To sacrifice Yourself to ensure,
The life of one, the one You seek,
A blessing You collect so deep.

To hear Your voice as it's words fade,
To watch Your lips as you're praying,
To hold Your hand for not another scar,
To wait for the one not afar.

To see your eyes as they blink,
The sad memories along with them sink,
New life yet again shall spring,
And born again Thy love shall sing.

Your Heart

A heart that never stops to cry,
A heart yet with such wings does fly,
A heart that never leaves my side,
A heart for one's love to reside.

My Life Ensured

It's hard for me to see Your face,
But with it's pain You do embrace,
The hardship life have You endured,
But life anew, to be ensured.

Come to Be

Gone again,
It chimes once more,
The pain, the strife has come to shore,
My heart is broken,
My soul unspoken,
Will it ever come to be!

Friend not Foe

To love someone is more than thought,
More than action, more than plot,
Love is from the heart,
From deep within,
A happy start, not weak, not thin.

Thinking of You makes me leap with joy,
A simple treasure I must employ,
Remember me from long ago,
I miss you deeply,
My friend, not foe!

Of My Heart

Remembering You has set me free,
Of my thoughts cannot try to flee,
Of my actions, ever grow,
Of my heart, to ever know.

Impossible to Ask

To tell one how much I miss You,
Would be an unbearable task,
More than one can imagine,
Something impossible to ask.

To say how much I love You,
Would be more than words can produce,
I miss You, my love, my everything,
Help me put my love to good use.

I'll be Your Key

Think of me when you're lonely,
Think of me when you're free,
Think of me when you're tired,
Think of me when you're weak.
Remember me when you feel hopeless,
When you're thoughts fly off with your heart,
Remember me when you're troubled,
And I will be your key, never to depart.

Always Above

When I was by the river, it made me think of
Your fluent love,
You care for me, and Your mercy,
Could come from only You above.
When I saw a star in the night sky,
It made me think of Your love,
And how it shines forever more,
Do I see it or not, it's always above.

How Beautiful

How beautiful, how wondrous, how mysterious
is Thy love.
How marvelous, how victorious, how gorgeous,
it shows that I can trust.
How amazing, how important, how
unpredictable, although You may be,
You're beautiful, You're loving, You intently
care for me.

A Delicate Rose

You remind me of a delicate rose,
So fragile, but gorgeous and pure,
Heavenly above other flowers,
A beauty to graciously endure,
A wonder to be explored,
By one so loyal and true,
A beautiful, ever pure rose,
A rose I give to You.

Special for You

If I were to grow a garden,
I would grow something for you,
I would plant it near the brook,
With the sunlight shining through.
I would plant it in fertile soil,
And water it every day,
It would grow so tall and beautiful,
And that rose just bloomed today.

Awake at Dusk

Waiting for the day to come,
When one day something would change,
An adventure to something I've never known,
Compared to where I am today.
Relying on what I know,
Which consists of faith and trust,
Waiting for the night to come, when waking elsewhere,
Awake at dusk.

What Your Smile Does

Listening for Your voice to calm,
And Your love, I feel on and on,
Your gentle smile spread over me,
This life, so real, is not a dream,
Of what I always wanted to know,
About Your caring heart even so,
To make me happy, and ever be,
An image of You,
A painting signed by Thee.

What I Feel

Although my pain gets the better of me,
I still want to live effortlessly,
Love seems to come with a price,
Even though it is free,
Ask Him, a new beginning to be.

The Most Beautiful

The birds chirping softly,
The flowers in their rows,
The moon, still hidden,
The sun now brightly shows,
The trees stretch to heaven,
Their leaves in summers green,
A truly beautiful world,
The most beautiful I have seen.

Slowly Escape

Once more, the moon arises,
The stars, to bright it's sky,
The quiet waters reflect,
It's path of light that shines,
Though dark, I feel such beauty,
The clouds don't hide it's face,
At dawn, to slowly fade,
Once more, to slowly escape.

To See Your Smiling Face

Awaiting the time of laughter,
Awaiting the time of peace,
A long time for sorrow,
Now, a time for belief.
What joy, now, that has come,
What love Thy have to bring,
To see the smiling faces,
To hear my dear friends sing.

Swiftly Turning

Seeing the windmills turning,
Ever so smooth from below,
Listening at night to the crickets,
Who only at nighttime show.
The stars some out with them, also,
The soothing air brings memories back,
This means the world to me,
Something I would miss to lack.

My Love for You

Looking off into the stars, my eyes see You
afar,
And with the sun that morning brings,
You still a-present are.
And when I am alone or afraid,
And wonder where to go,
My heart is led through meadows of green,
My love for You does grow.

In His Sight

Although the path is winding,
The branches hide it's way,
Although the night is falling,
Stars to end it's day.
Although the birds stop singing,
And owls rehearse for night,
Although you feel so lonely,
I know you're in God's sight.

Wings to Fly

Your love, as numerous as the stars or sand
upon the shore,
The care that comes from up above could not
be treasured more.
But when I think about you,
Your heart that beauty shows,
Your love gives me wings to fly,
Wings to guide my soul.

Intent Beauty

The snow comes down so softly,
It's delicate patterns amaze,
I watch the beauty intently,
My eyes upon them gaze.
Covering the trees in its whiteness,
The cold subdued by the light,
I watch the sun hide slightly,
And to it I say goodnight.

A Delicate Disguise

I wake up in the morning,
And watch the sun to rise,
It warms the winter air,
And shades a delicate disguise,
Oh when it falls again,
The night, that is, to sleep,
I watch the moon to come,
And greet the midnight deep.

Throughout the Air

I love to watch the birds,
Fly throughout the air,
For me, a troubled task,
For them, a simple care,
To hear their songs begin,
So soft, yet every sweet,
For me, not as courageous,
For them, a never ending elite.

The Clock

Back and forth he paces,
On and on he sounds,
Every hour more cases,
Of the heavy bounds,
Here and there I catch him,
Now and then I see,
His hand waving beyond the glass,
I stare at him, he stares at me.

Again I Watch You Smile

Amazing how it happens,
How friends become to see,
The beauty of each other,
The simple similarities.
Again, I watch you smile,
Again I miss to see,
When I'm away for a time,
How far I feel from thee.

I Watch the Trees

Above, I watch the trees,
They may seem to be alike,
But when I look more closely,
I understand the sight.
So different, may they be,
Their branches aligned so far,
I watch the bending beauty,
And the nests between them are.

Endless Waves

One more time I call,
Upon the open sea,
It's waves rolling in the wind,
My hair blowing behind me.
It's warm boundaries found,
The sun to keep it's right,
Again I call so far,
No echoes to come back, nor sight.

Again to Bloom

Come again, oh wind of love,
That passes by my window,
Please come again, oh rising sun,
That not till night shall dwindle,
Will you come again? Oh moon that shines
down to light my room.
Do come again, new morning light,
And start again to bloom.

Beautiful Spring

Sweet sound of rain upon the roof,
The ongoing spring routine,
Bring sun to shine upon the plants that beauty
to us bring.
Oh come, flawless birds that paint the sky,
That sing to us with delight,
And then they fly away till morning,
While the owls occupy the night.

Song upon the Wind

Sweet sound of song upon the wind,
Soft voices do I hear.
A whisper here and there I catch,
The panting of the deer.
I cannot understand their words,
Nor can they say for me,
But I can sense their being,
And I can see their unique beauty.

Free Again

So free again, I now do feel,
A life that used to be empty,
But now, what does to me appeal,
A heart to love relenting.
Again the soft wind makes me smile,
Once more my happiness has no denial,
Forever Your love will overflow, will compile,
You are so special to me.

Out the Crystal Window

I look out the crystal window,
I see the rolling fields,
Upon them grow tall the trees,
That beauty to us yields.
So grasping is the sight,
So simply, purely, unique.
No flaws, no mistakes, no troubles,
Nothing, ever, to critique.

Your Beauty Within

If you were in my garden,
You would be the prettiest fair,
Your tall magnificence would tower,
The gloom and all despair.
Your petals so delicate and soft,
Your stem uniquely strong and prim,
The beauty I see outwardly,
Reflects the beauty within.

Gently Glittering

So intriguing are the waters,
Full of life, not death,
Oh, softly rolling waters,
That nothing hindered does possess.
The sun, full of beauty,
The moon at night to keep.
Oh gently glittering waters,
Your glories never complete.

Quickly Past

Quickly past, the seasons go,
Not missing anything in-between,
I watch the difference between the snows,
And the difference between the spring.
I see the leaves of fall, the snow that winter
brings,
The sweet smell that spring bestows, and the
birds in summer sings.
My heart watching these beautiful seasons,
The change between the four,
The love you feel together,
The love, forever more.

Blossom to Be

One time I saw a snowflake,
It's crystal patterns amaze,
The cold of winter bellows,
Among the new-year days.
And then, I saw a flower,
Soon about to bloom,
It's petals spreading widely,
The stem so tall assume.
Soon after, the trees were giving,
Sending their leaves abroad,
Their colors so bright and cheery,
Through the winding trails I trod.
And here again is the snowflake,
Falling slowly, I see,
I wait again for springtime,
For that budding blossom to be…

In the Sky

Once more I sing, once more I cry,
Your sun shines brightly in the sky,
Again I pray,
Again I see,
Your everlasting true beauty!

Ever True

A simple flower,
Yet a significant gift,
A symbol of hope for the life yet to live.
The curving petals,
And drops of dew,
Such a pure beauty,
And sign ever true.

A True Treasure

Free again,
A beauty revealed,
Skipping across a newly bloomed field.
A cliff of wonder,
A mist of pleasure,
Every moment on that mountain,
Is a true treasure.

Tall Twin Towers

A bend in the path,
Lined with flowers,
The trees full of life,
Like tall twin towers.
A way to you, it must surely be,
A place I hope, eternally.

No Darkness Lies

A clear window of life,
Before my eyes,
There, in the mist no darkness lies.
Flowers speckled all about,
The hills, winding tall and stout.
A view of life,
A simple pleasure,
I hope I'll see that sight forever.

Sealed and Signed

A tunnel of truth,
An ocean of love,
A clear sunny sky when you look up above.
A rocky foundation,
Yet a special kind,
God's own artwork,
Sealed and signed.

A Star in the Sky

A beautiful symbol, a star in the sky,
A foreign image one cannot deny,
A sign of love, a sign of rebirth,
A Baby in a manger, a King of all worth.

Three men traveled far, to see this great King,
The star to far lead them, the angels to sing,
Three gifts have they brought, three hearts to
bestow,
Through the day, through the night, through the
blizzards and snow.
The straw brushed His face,
As the white did the earth,
The angels as bright
As the star leading the search.

A manger to hold Him, as He sleeps in the hay,
No troubles to wake Him, that cold Christmas
day,
The three there now giving, the true way to live,
He was receiving, showing us to give.

Fall will never Know

Spring, it always find its way through the winter days,
The sun sweetly shining, the beauty of its rays,
Oh come! The birds who nest, between the tall-grown birch,
Oh come! The flowers who sing, among the weeds they search,
They search for rain to fall, upon the petals that flow,
They search for freedom of life, that fall will never know.

Your Love never Fails

Before the sadness had gone away,
Before the night had left,
Before the clouds had hid the light,
Before the stars had kept,
Beyond the skies a hope that brought,
Beyond the love that ceased to stop,
Although we thought that all was lost,
Your love has never failed.

About the Author

Grace Rapavi lives in Jackson, Wisconsin. She enjoys the outdoors, music, and many sports- including watching her favorite team the Green Bay Packers. She loves animals and has a puppy named Blitz.